*AIRS*

## Also by Maurice Scully

### Books
*Love Poems & Others*
*5 Freedoms of Movement*
*The Basic Colours*
*Priority*
*Steps*
*Livelihood*
*Sonata*
*Tig*
*Doing the Same in English*
*Humming*
*A Tour of the Lattice*
*Several Dances*
*Play Book*
*Things That Happen*

### Booklets
*Prior*
*Certain Pages*
*Over & Through*
*Prelude, Interlude & Postlude*
*Tree with Eggs*
*Work*
*Game On*

### Art Object
*Numbers* [with Coracle Press]

### e-chapbooks
*Five Dances*
*Rain* [signed piece]
*Plays*

### CD
*Mouthpuller*

### Children's
*What is the Cat Looking At?*

# Maurice Scully

# *AIRS*

Shearsman Books

First published in the United Kingdom in 2022 by
Shearsman Books Ltd
PO Box 4239
Swindon
SN3 9FN

Shearsman Books Ltd Registered Office
30–31 St. James Place, Mangotsfield, Bristol BS16 9JB
(this address not for correspondence)

www.shearsman.com

ISBN 978-1-84861-801-5

Copyright © Maurice Scully, 2022
The right of Maurice Scully to be identified as the author
of this work has been asserted by her in accordance with the
Copyrights, Designs and Patents Act of 1988.
All rights reserved.

ACKNOWLEDGEMENTS

*Blackbox Manifold, Cyphers, Golden Handcuffs Review,
Oystercatcher, Stinging Fly, Tears in the Fence, Trinity Today*

*AIRS*

## TRACKING

You take them differently
first by dense focus & rereading
then floating focus & rereading
then dense focus again
then rereading here & there
then sifting & weighing
then comparing & weighing
then rejecting
then accepting again
on different terms
& in part
deepening the picture
superimposing each reading
as you go carrying them along
lightly but comprehensively
in the small white notebook
under the olive tree on the table
beside a handful of olives
& a few leaves from the same tree
in the shadows moving in the
breeze in the sunlight
beside a white house outside a
village by the sea & – well –
you might as well live.
The apple I picked picked me
ticked poetry poetry picked it
& I picked poetry & skipped
with it till it fell to my
palm & filled it plump
to the skin it seemed orbiting
as it turned – tick –

with its turning heart
flitting through mirrors to the
back of the mind so that
pluck that string reacting
in the afternoon up
in the middle of a city
by the sea reaching
to where light
while light lasts nicks
hollows flickers
shadowing your still
papers & set it down there
by the pen on your desk
& the work.

# MIRRORS

*Whisper-whisper*
go the little
branches

overhead in the wind
hitting each other
& trickling into

the map in yr pocket
mountains rivers ravines
falling together

sideways through life
down all of it all over
again. *Wake up!*

Patterns of
empty spaces
placed

together

apart

blue glare.
Matt black.

Did you get those
seeds I sent from
Lesotho by the way?

Turn round, bow.

He is dead now.

Suddenly one
morning early in
Soria

a blur of
brightly-coloured
figures

in the distance
in a park …

& following them
their colours grew
& their numbers

too & excitement
streaming from
street

to street
down to
the centre

& the main square
& Machado
on a chair

beside his
child-bride
quiet …

the Festival of
the Virgin of
Guatemala

dancing in a
bowing &
swaying

looping &
bowing motion
two steps

forward
one
step

back

while the band
flowed &
swayed

blowing a
short repetitive
melody

how
small
a part

yes dipping &
swaying forward-
&-back

a little
off-key too
how

small a part they/
mirrors/splintery
bits of

mirror/yes/
to our
ears

how small a
part (of time)
we share

the doll-witch-
mother-virgin
effigy

but gracefully –

shimmering cloak,
black wig, glass tiara,
plastic skulls …

The elephant
in the room
is the elephant.

## AIR

down

through
noiseless
breezes

fall
gently
from

the trees
again

down

turning
in grace-

ful contact

slowly

turning

in a
warmer
upthrust

up too
    & sideways
light

then down

landing
in place again
without a I

went back
to/work I
dust rising

silver
& green
outside

went back
to
I

lifting

turning pages
shifting
boxes

3342

to get to
this
piece of –

persistent
piece of –
whose

birthday
is it anyway
(dark)

& what
is it to/
what

is it
*time*
to

442231

(now)

throw
away
next? –

this
persistent
piece of –

darkness –

darkness
on yr
desk

a splash zone
round a
crater

that sound of –
hold still –
*failure* is it? …

*whisper-whisper*
go the
terminally

envious
in a sudden
run of

pent
malice.

.

that's it – decades – doctorates –
centuries
of the

woven babble
of the species –
let

the honey-
combing
begin

*cada
mañana hago
mi*

*cama* then
squirt a
splash of

Death's Door
estate bottled
darkly rich

its
black blood
hit bottom

as gates – windows –
bang in the
storm

(berry – fig – leather)
giving the
wind

its energy back –
threatening delighting
advising cajoling & –

scribble
scribble

shiver of richness –
fine-tasting
poison –

almost ripping yr roof off.

dusk. disturbance
among the
blackbirds. night.

.

& so dear god the 19th century
melts into
the 20th

the 20th into the 21st
rain-damaged –
useless –

but keeping shape
while you slept
then radiates &

radiates & *radiates* &
believing (grieving)
(feeling) radiates

& (erasing, retrieving)
radiates &
(watching

attending) (wondering
absorbing) (re-
imagining &

un-remembering)
stressed links in a
chain of stories

(*turn that page now!*)
(&) sorrowing
too

(flickering antennae
a dot stopped
on a

lower leaf) & – through
a thin break
in the mist –

radiates still.
what then is your
castle made of?

blank.

& your garden?

fallen apple-shell
where a bird
had fed.

*salut!*

.

sinking back
into the
bed

the soft
the sweet

thinking she said for
long for happy
for

murmuring o
bent over
you

o pouring love
for so for
soft

for what *is*
this stuff for
you o

love o
love for
you

*tang art*
*tang*

pungent-dazzle-
leaf-touch-
thrill!

.

that rumble
of rhetoric
(click-clack)
that whisper

of the actual – that.
*quick march!* heel. turn.
erase. click. where?
click. there. air?

spare it.
not another
word.
.

*oyé!*
*Carmen! – José! –*
down through the little village –
late & dark –

down into the
twisting streets
nobody thinking –

threading – really to
sleep here this
time of year

luxuriate
instead in
the

slight cool
of night
whose

chance-breath-breezes
play silk against
the skin –

& overhead –
*stars!* – a
pulsing avalanche …


.


*of course*
*there'll always be*
*a reason to be*

*happy somehow.*
somehow. if
the ground of

being is
threaded
through

to the name
of the thing
as part of

the eman-
ation of
the thing

anterior to
the naming of it
so that

emanation
& name re-awaken
enwound

each thing
thus woven as
thing-perceived …

dot in a
vast network
each itself

a
mere
dot

in a single arm
of a single
galaxy

in a sea of
billions
among

which
worlds in which
life in which

this violent overactive
species moving
in to kill …

put yr scrap
in the panicle
anyway

a dead leaf
dancing in
the breeze

descending
quietly
down

then up a
little then
down again

this
way
that

through
time

time-in-light
& space-
in-time

to
here.

## EARTH

Pulled on sock first one foot
in the winter cold then the other
*ti-tum* queynt chasms &

phantasms of rhetoric *tum-ti*
so the big toe doesn't go through
the new hole in it (oh well) then

fiddling with fiddly laces placed
towel on rad brushed hair challenged
the mirror opened the door stepped out.

Fab! What would Milton have Satan say?
(This is a poem, right?) Pegasus, the keynote
speaker this year, delivered a stunningly

astringent paper on '*The Definitions of Light*' –
vivid splash of blossom, dark alleyway
in a city, we opened our notebooks, & …

    looking
    into a
    slim

    script
    on
    yellow-

    ing vell-
    um following
    the hand of a/

the mis-
transcriptions
&

the/

I   or   land/

spots of
crushed glass/

time to put your work aside
then tip-tap to
anyway to

dammit walk up
to stamp in fact
up

that path up
to and slam
the

gate with a bang
and head
out.

Up.

For good.

Of course.

Love is …

Caught in a
shaft of early
sunlight

once a butterfly
flew over
a wall

over a
reservoir
scattering

influence
over
us

dot and
then dot and
then a dot …

the God That
Thunders (*and*
Re-Thinks)

so that –
that was that.
Now then.

Connect!

*shivering a leaf a  
on a  
breeze made visible  
shivering  
a leaf  
on a branch  
in a  
breeze made visible  
once by  
shivering  
a leaf on a branch made  
a breeze  
visible shivering  
one one one one one*

# DICE

Thing is I don't remember much & what I think I do I
suspect is muddled & inaccurate by ordinary standards ... so.
Fiction fills fiction to make fiction: fix *that* if you can.

Your question was not a problem, why should it be, listen to it,
listen to it rumbling underground, the problem's elsewhere, release from
immediate worry, intricate progress of worries – the question was:
dark. Dark.

I knew you thirty years ago. You passed with your wife & child
& friend. Busy. Happy. I passed: *we* passed. You'd been moving
towards the Reward Storage Terminal all that time. I'd been
making for the Periphery. I didn't know. Sunlight on a leaf.
Histories. The weight of that.

A cobweb fissure in her heart of glass through which some bright liquid
pulses rhythmically backlit by the future (been there, dark too) squirt-squirt.
Sit down, son. Have I ever told you about *poetry*?

Thing is I don't remember much & what I think I do ...

In these scales then – as we weigh things – as they emerge & grow –
    & weigh them – fragmented rag-time
        at the end of the garden
    memories   dependable/undependable   disturbances
across air &
    coming & going
      over time-spaces
        a river of glinting ripples
    flowing into the Best  & we weigh them
           & the days slip by

        flowing into the Best
                the Best Progressive

the Future Perfect
           the Perfect

    the Best Perfect Progressive

            Worst Conditional

    into the Dark Simple    & we weigh them    by capillary action

stone     paper     birdcall     fibre     lichen     root.

# SONG

Into the canopy
around a trunk
a stem
twists up
into the light
& sprouts
heart-leaves
light green
nestled among dark
moving each move
sighing for pleasure
sinking back into
she over/he/colour
for happy shade for
fear dapple for
rest amen there
is sunshine then
rain.

At the end of a page
you're older – a pulse
of light slipping
along a thread –
*it must be love (love, love)*
though an off-key chorus
of optimistic wish-babble
won't get you a ticket
on the train Tuesday
building o
a stem around a
trunk twists up

in to where
stories pleat
complete a pleasure
& tighten into each other
to open a throat
in the storm.

## SCALES

Crumpled
paper napkin with a base
pattern of gardening implements,
their names in pale
ink, pale circular
coffee stains where
a cup was placed
repeatedly,
the 17th.

Great floppy racemes
dangling from every branch
drenched in scent
over the surface of a pond
dotted with petals
where fish-ripples as they land
ripple upside-down cloud-wisps
sliding past in warm air…
Fixed on a flatbed offset press
using hand-drawn positives
on translucent plastic you
dip this piece here then
twist that, mix & start. Now.

Is that a mistake? Pen pauses over paper,
does/*that feelin grab you deep inside
& send you reelin where yr love
can't hide & then go stealin through the*/
flatten it! work that matt square
until it gets to/left to/dark, spiky
angular, splotched.

It's your birthday again
far, far in the future &
you're g(h)o/(st)ing your
way back past the
Temple of the Puny Penis,
Church of the Scaredy-Cat
Art, Chapel of the 5
Miserly Mistakes,
bladder senna, incense dust,
scroll fragments, gravy trains,
slow-flowing traffic
through neo-baroque hyper-splashes
towering over an
arterial avenue
& gigantic crystal pyramids
of glinting logic
in the distance –
just to say *Hi!*

## BEING THERE

Gauzy cloud under blue
over low blue hills:
make a map
then walk through it, tilt that
idea to one side
to feel the breeze
(the breeze feels you)
push a space between
the weeds of the day
take a small cool stone in yr hand.
If a fleck of paper caught
in a bent staple in silence
is a node of language
& learning a language without
the Learning Stomp –
changes what? – tapping fingers
quietly to quite a different
rhythm – changes the air you see through –
a scratch on your hand healing,
a fly go past …
yellow stones on yellow clay
where a yellow butterfly alights,
deeper-shaded, visible.
It may be so.

## TRANSLATING

As the narrow stone street
descends steeply
first diagonally to the left then
straight for a bit
then sharply to the right
under a protruding wrought-iron rainspout
some local blacksmith has expended
quite a bit of exuberance hammering out
down
to the main
road & the river
this village –
chill, trim –
stays
can you see it?
in all of Spain
by fine mountains
under wide skies
drifting buzzards
migrating cranes –
still stays still
completely
still.

Some moth
species can
pick up
the sonar
probings of
a bat &
instantly

close their
wings in
flight to
drop like
a stone to
the ground.
That's it.
Exactly.
Nobody here?
Well now.

## LOOK

Take a surface shaving
& pierce it with your
pen happy Mr

Happy white male
European anglophone
hiberno-trickle person

hi there mister in the hotel
mirror bring your privileged
bones nearer if you

dare live another
day be ready fat &
standard issue educated.

Click. Flash. As soon as
you can. Prithee hark!
I flick a coin; its glint

flicks me: heads tails
fangs money. Rose up then
the threatened Authority

of the old Academy to
defend the Dissemination
of Pine Nuts to Several

tribal doctors throughout
the Islands of the Red.
There goes that cat across

the roof again. That's
the thing. Ribbed grip
of your pen, shimmer

of paper, open oblong,
its whispered reception,
its needle-point poised

to trace, to r(wr)i[gh]t(e)
it all down quite clearly.
Didn't expect that. Did they?

# NIGHT STUDIO

Room quiet, house quiet, shadows
follow your hand as your pen follows
along a page, shadowed, quiet – mycelium,
night, mountains, darkness. Apples
fringed with leaves on a pale plate on a table
in the place you find yourself now are … Stop.
Translate: they float, they dazzle, they
stay quite still though still full of those tiny
granules of unrestricted dance-tilt whispering
their colours into each other & each adjacent
object of domestic presence, different
from, far from, far indeed from what you
know, so don't imagine you do. Welcome!
Still. That's what they do.

# CHEQUERED AIR

Listen, for clues.
Look up. Swap,
snatch – what?
Reddish glow of
withered needles
on a lopped conifer
by an old stone wall
along which slide
filmy shadows
lost in conversation
rippling over finely
fit-together blocks –
monk – urchin –
blacksmith – card-sharp –
hundreds of years ago
among the fortifications
of a cragtop castle
overlooking a plain
in the sun. Strong sun.
Long time ago.
Passing through.
Catching the light,
holding it, returning it,
hearing a fly
land on a rock,
the pen loaded,
the afternoon quiet,
sepals flung back
for pollination,
root-fibres active
underground in the dark.

I was wiping some dust
off my glasses
absent-mindedly cleaning
the lenses & looking up
suddenly saw grey sky
rainspots on windowglass
& a few seagulls wheeling
over the rooftops opposite.
That's how it is. Black.
White. Then a train.
Then a figure
under trees
moves away into
the distance, listen –
whisper of the pen
on the page –
how does that one go
the one about
*The Simple Life?* –
a whirr of wings, look up,
bright black eye
of the robin
sideways, checking,
surrounded by,
steeped in, silence.
Your move.

# A GREY AREA

To make a table you need to be able to exploit the fable
of the re-useable – wood, seed, flower, song – & not dabble
too long in the sound of the hammer & the saw: phrases, lines,
naval terminology. Are you at sea here? No fear: rhyme is
unable to cake a gunwale at this latitude. Read the label.

In my copy of the discussion of the fragmentary Berlin parchments
of Sappho's lyrics in Hugh Kenner's *The Pound Era* read decades ago
now some parts of words are blanked by a production glitch thus:
"The Gree     ords do in a general way hang together, though no one is
   re     sure what some of them are … " What are the odds?

## TABLED

An apple
with a bite
on its red

side showing
white going
(slowly)
brown

slipping downhill
past the lip of
another hill

to the
coast by
the trees &
shops

in whispery
little movements
a cup there
on the table

round a corner
rooftop satellite
dishes & dishes
to hand here

too then

click.

Red pouring over green
green shimmering underneath
bruising where the fall hit grass
perforations where birds fed
glistenings where a snail had been
shadow-agitations where the flower was,
stem curved, light at the tip
where sprouting from its dimple it catches
*have-have had-had having-having cannot-have*
*could-not-have would-not-have can!*
sing the little birds now feeding
among the branches overhead.

.

    That my children
    will not be caught
    in a world-wide web.

    *Click* goes a crow
    *limit-limit*
    a sparrow

    woke into
    the adventure
    out of the blue

    a hand writing a book
    long lines tiny script
    fluently unwinding

art
art & flowers art &
trees & flowers & all –

take that apple up
& put it down
again

glisten of the bitten,
firm border
of the skin.

When the distinctly
vicious meet
the distinctly

vulnerable & stick
the knife in deep &
clean for kudos

(& financial gain)
& their followers
sky-rocket

& fans whirr over
that picnic when
blood drips

audibly onto the stopped
machine & the machines
stop.

What can be done?

.

A new stamp shows
the head of Einstein.
Kid in post office asks:
"Is it Dracula?"

In Orkney the snipe
is called a
"water-pleep".

## DO RE MI

Travelling north towards the mountains
in the softly undulating bus when out of the blue
that sound
once so common, rare now
the crisp turning of a page
in a seat behind you
someone reading
reading a book
a paper book
a new page.

The sound of the loosening of the bolt to open the door –
that bit of language.

The sound of the door closing, that.

Sound of your pen thinking.

Fingers on a page.

A page turned.

Storks migrating at such great height … audible calls.

Putting the kettle on to heat water for tea
to heat the body on a cold spring morning
in the mountains, warm the heart.
A dark rectangle on a pale sheet, prose (a dark
stream in a pale crevasse, poetry?) Disappearance of
the last piece of money. Here we are then you say
when you don't mean "here" & don't know "we".
The spread of language over the world.

# CHINK

But those double images always
remained mysterious      how?

pictures         intensity

translatable into

outside the words the

sound peels off the poetry

crumbled

on the floor

of the empty

gallery. Echo. A dust.

That's it.

But not quite.

Is this then that bright outline of a matrix,
of a "radiating primacy of the invisible"
that I used to contemplate, wide-eyed,
blind, in kindergarten-college for the tubby
drunken hero-professor? I lift a finger & notice
a star outside a window in a space of fictional
energy it seems/dreams he must now hand
over to you, you there taking that last step
beginning your descent by the backstairs to

the alleyway below. Sirens, lights. A field of
weaving energies that peels off, softly descending
to cover a corner of your precious western
imagination a moment then dissolve into
the brainstem. NFS.

Yes. Maybe.

Maybe. Yes.

# SELF-PORTRAIT AS ODDITY

Good when a branch scrapes the roof of your shed
in the wind at night, tapping and telling, saying
good, good to be alive, good to hear, tell, remember,
projéct, good just to sit down and listen in the dark.

Tear it up and start again.

Knurled brass god-monster, allegoric figure of persistent stress,
grins through fissure in roof at Struggling Writer at Desk. Pale
moon-print shock. Go Struggle, Boy! Thus Hope, done as a
laughing statue and set on a green dome in high, bright light, over
the majestic gates to the city, cameras affixed, each fidget, each
shadow, each crimp in the world-sheet, each suppressed wail of
their cars on the trail policed; granite. And that's that.

.

Then suddenly ... Suddenly your birth-date prints – moist to
paper – lips together after some tart quip – ink on a turning
roll – its dash narrowing, arrowing forward, forward to your
death-date, then stopped before a little white space, glistening –
that other – the melodrama of this secret printing ...

Tear it up, and start again.

What gouges your wax today, what light falls on which
encrustations of ego-shell now? Good question! Thanks. So.
Turn this monument around, have a good look. The Department
of Special Pleading still thrives, I see. And the Secret Department
of Constant Money-Worry.

Good.

Climb the stairs to the light. Off this landing
many sub-Departments of Ratified Aesthetic Delight.
Language, the Tangible World. Art.

Further up we have a small pool of Philosophy
(greatly depleted) and at the top, living tip of this
Curiosity is its Turbine of Incessant, Coherent (*hah!*)
Note-Taking.

Splashes. Sparks.

> *A child-bed on a narrow landing*
> *by a little deep-set window on the dark.*
> *Yr uncles in the next room discussing tomorrow's*
> *weather in bed. It is sixty years ago. On a farm.*
>
> *I am five. Snails move over an old pan outside.*
> *The yard is black. A tree shifts. Everybody is*
> *dead now, except this voice here talking to you,*
> *to you, to this, to let you know a sort of happiness,*
> *despite everything, yes – a yellow claw descends,*
> *a hen clucks & blinks – a kind of human mist*
> *is drifting across that place somehow*
> *to here. I hear it. Feel-hear it. Here it is.*

Good.

.

Good when a branch scrapes the roof in the wind at night
tapping and telling, humming *good – good to be alive,*

*good to hear, tell, remember, projéct, good just to sit down and listen in the dark.*

# IMPRINTS

An earthworm knows by taste which end of a twinned pine needle to drag into its burrow first.

For an instant, the water froze into an image of a ploughed field or perhaps a meadow – then reverted. Behind the boat, the wake tumbled & roared, a chaotic, ceaseless white tumult, occasionally spitting bullets of icy spray past our faces. Further out to sea, close to that vague horizon in the distance, in the mist, shapes & lights of vast freighters could be seen, moving steadily on.

I walk through the streets of an unfamiliar town. It's snowing & growing darker. The streets I am following become less & less well lit. Our old house is on one of the last streets. Farther off it is already the countryside. There is a bar across from the house. I go in & order a bottle of wine. I am the only customer. A painter I once knew used to say *all art is collage.* He was right.

The earthworm knows by taste …

# A TILTED MIRROR

How many times?
Which cliff? If I
give you this will
you give me that?

Blackbirds nesting
in the fork of a
tree behind a
house

in a weave of
beautiful music
in the early
middle ages

before the black
death hit & cholera
& war &
localized famine

over a dog
doing its nut
down there

in the backyard
beside a midden
with an old white
kettle in it smile

scowl grimace
is skittle bawn
morgay on

you know
the repertoire
rainpools
dust-pockets

what must it
have been like
though to hear such
reading-murmur

daily/nightly
in the greenish
half-light
as a norm

warm &
human

through a short life oh
forgetting everything
beginning again

clean slate
held pen
the whole shebang
scratching

out mistakes
to re-write with
precision on
precious vellum

the words of a god.
A god. *The* god.

*Boom!* goes
the thunder
through the air

then a little rain
growing quieting
growing again

your door
swinging open
in the breeze

closing again
thunder-crackle
(more flashes)

& opening
rain spattering
the parched …

the dust …
then suddenly
venting its

force in a
kind of
luminous dark

the storm's
vertical whips
lash the twin

hills of the village
in waves
terraces awash

spouting rushing
gushing through
downpipes

gutters rooftops
ledges flowing
down

*rivering* down
the little streets
until it

passes into quiet
a blue-grey dark.
Peace.

Distant rumble.
Distant …
distance.

## CARDS

Five for Sorrow
Three to the
Shriven Joker

who can forget
the female to
the male

when worlds
collide & splash
& nobody's

the same again
as roots change
orientation &

leaves laugh –
Queen of Hurricane
Ace of Calm.

The girl to the boy
kissing
the boy to the girl

giving – giving –
Queen of Reception
Little Jack All-Heart

beginning of
the shock of
delight. Given.

Never the same
again quite never
to be the same again

beech leaves
tickled together
in the air overhead

Five for Delight Ten
for Darkness-taken-
again-apart-&-then.

O all the career-moves
all the tricks &
works

all the
interviews &
CV-flarings from the

adult hammered-
together World
dropped

through
a chute (what's
the point

of the name of
the namer if
sludge-think

ink-pool?) &
pouring out to
sea!

Not travelling
back in time
pushing

time back
through time
so that they

telescope &
elide like
that.

It's funny how/
It's important
that/It could

be true if/
On the other
hand when/

crowns angels
cowrie shells
marks

Tanzanian
shillings

honey set
to crystal
dice click

dance-tilt
slap table
echo then
　show.

## ARC

Wipe glasses
sip tea
what *is* this anyway
(*teach a little*
*breathe a*
*little live a little*
*breathe a little*
*slip a little – touch-*
*touch-touch*) it's
called … It's
Saturday. 4.56 pm.
Log that dog's yapping
in the laneway
following each line around
& about &
then down
      again
& about &
*then* start: this
must this must
be

   moved glasses-case
   to the left then heard a
   click outside

must be

   each tree a spectral
   sheath of rising moisture
   each forest a colony

    of gleaming spirits
    in the transpiration
    stream glinting &
    clicking between
    base & open sky

this must be –

    the tube of the pen
    its cylinder lying along the
    spine of the notebook –

look

    be that beautiful little quick
    feathered animal feeding by
    the wave-edge here
    just recently arrived
    migrating all of five thousand
    miles to here    here

must be can
history collapse
on itself
bend once
twice
still wild
out of the
mind's world
this must be
*idir na*
in some sense
a coin that

manoeuvres
the air up
& back –
flick –
down to
threading finely
to base
fitting shape into
shadowhood
floating somehow
somehow fluid
somehow
pre-prepared –
      art
*idir na*
*idir na daoinibh duarca*
this must be art.

## PITCH

In that odd book
with two covers
one within the other
take a look:

Monday, & a tiny cone
from a conifer
drops to the ground.
Breathe in air.

Pass your hand over
the outline of the
next question.
Is it sound?

How many books fall
together into waste?
How strange this solo
experiment is.

Are you afraid?
Are you
understanding
history?

Who is that watching
the watcher now? And
what do you call that?

In this book you
spend your life writing
the pages the pages
repeat and sing.

Stone fibre lichen root.

Caught out
playing the Wise Man
the Fool stealthily
the Strangler Fig

border zones
great spaces
biding tight
in the storm's eye –

your home.

## TUNING

… then began taking notes
writing *lost roads* for *crossroads* (my mistake)
to which I believed myself then
to be approaching (*plus ça change!*)
under a ripple
of some persistent distant house alarm
in the wind
singing pinging a repetitive air
on air through air airily
mechanical for sure
for you      & you & you & you & you
the way
fruit depends from its branch
in its function – take me, eat me, spread my seed –
or that habit
developed in cultivars
to cluster under leaf-cover
to be harvested before birds get to them yes
certain species
raspberries for instance
delicious
a pleasant introvert
who moved quietly in
several
intersecting
social
circles
to make a table you need a cable on your tugboat
before the music
on O'Connell Street
against the wind & the sleet

before the music
began – one, two –
odd really –
*h'mmm* …

## LULLABY

In a pool of light
two books used to
prop a third
under the
extended light-cone
of the lamp
in the dark
of a stormy night
in February
near the sea
layer over layer
quiet inside
settling into
work again
cascades
patterns
a neat fit –
grammars expanded –
jelly lichens
that contain
nostoc
a cyanobacteria
instead of
algae …
that after-rain calm
that spatters
your shed-roof
in the cold
helping your mind along
through the trees
their typo-happy canopies

in sunlight
shimmering
under the hills
over there where
you remember now that
viscosity is
measured in time
in units of
poise.

## CANVAS

She smoked sixty cigarettes a day
worked through the night if she felt like it
gave money to friends
neglected the washing up
collected broken pieces of china
& loved Elizabethan poetry.
Her favourite painter was Rubens
whose sumptuous female models
she somewhat resembled.
Not seeing the point of putting cat food on a plate
she simply emptied the cans on to the kitchen floor.
She never locked her car
ignoring all advice
including medical advice.
About government, current affairs & rational discussion
she remained headily aloof.

    wondrous this wallstone
            giantwork crumbled
    towers tumbled
            rime on lime

Let's see now … where was I?

Before one can enjoy the fruits of living one must free oneself
of certain crippling liabilities – the fear of gods, the fear of death
& the fear of damnation – lay these ancient ghosts once & for all!
Come on Epicurus, Lucretius. Greed, murder, envy, self-pity,
suicide, treason & common betrayal.

A
small
black fly
walks up the page
through the letter
*h*
in 'behaviour'
then flies away
to land again
on the margin of the facing page
opposite the word
'resisting'
thread-like antennae
waving
then off again
to land on the
middle finger
of my
non-writing hand.

# FRAME

trees drop raindrops bigger
than previously (though the rain has stopped)
& vertical too – look up –
pellets of their cloud-love
plummet to yr moving boot-top
to splash into bits
on the grass, one hits
yr face, cold, & the trees laugh
you into place & down the back of yr neck
in the shadows to the fibrous roots
feeling the impossible
happen in the plot long ago
if you don't know the language then
tough luck stand back

# MAP 1

Vertebrae
skull-bits
dog-bones

pig; our
plastic brains –
a midden –

art, pen, notebooks,
desk, heater humming
in the dead of winter

& so on
down
to

sip
to the beat of
a single drop

(dot)
mid-air
into

the sink-top
tea under the
window

(rubble-adjustments
honey-profit
love-shares) …

Keep.
Amass.
Grip.

You, are here.

# MAP 2

The wind hits the wall
the wall holds the wind
the wind licks, kisses, bites
every crevice every smooth bit
hard (pause) & hard again.
The wall stays put in this.
This is its song.
This is not the end of anything.
This is a song. Dark, & a
glitter of yellow streetlights
an owl's face so designed
they say as to catch
the sound of its prey
its silent *a-b-c* flight
to help it hear it
in the dark grass down there
not so much as not
to be heard as
*word-word-word-word-word.*

# MAP 3

When my brother
died
suddenly
I read the two books
he had been reading
at the time.
To finish them for him.
From his bedside table.
Curiously (or not) I knew both writers
I mean, personally
and.

## WORKING

Working round an aperture in silence
a ground silence against which to mark time
this tender bridge (take care)   deeper in
a deep breath
this tender bridge between here &

over there
crystal tinkle of birdsong
filaments & dots drifting on red
under your eyelids in the sun
here where an arrow of sunlight
highlights fine detail on a ceramic tile
beside you, kissing it in fact, here it is,
simple, across vast, across a vast, here,
touch it, a thin layer, puckered …

   the character
      of April
  is different from
      the character
  of the Margin of
      the Calendar
  in May.

  Birds map
     a food place
  establish
  a table
     & more
  just in case.

       Facts' vanishing-points
              peppered parentheses
                       sudden blanks.

    Make a list.

Then back to work hey-ho dust rising, pages turning, shifting boxes to get to this persistent point through this mound of useless … this piece of darkness on your desk to work with.

## MAPPING

Shiver of a leaf in a breeze, a hammer
hitting a bell on a steeple-top in the square
now to place this little town (now) with
emphatic precision by the down-at-heel
palace here, now. I put my cup down.
Whose house is that?

Hollows, pockets, shadows, lines, stitches,
pins & needles & the times taken to patch
sunlight to countless little threads distinct
on a chair in a room upstairs somewhere
over a garden on the northern edge of a
coastal city: quiet.

Draw a line through that then add them up.
Once upon a time. Becoming included in its
future the tracing of a straight line out from
a point in the past along this side of flickering
presence with the aid of a Ruler only reproduces

the straight line already constructed along the
ruler's edge. What is your house made of then?
Tapping hammer, dove-blur in a tree by a
bedroom window, travelling water through
pipes about a wall, purline, gable. Birdcall.

Your jacket on the back of a chair.

## AS THE CAT

Patterns in a
book open
on a
table

gold/black
gold/green
gold/gold

that make
your I
mean have
your name

inscripted
in it.
      Crisp.
(*Crap!*)

No.

Rewind that.

Trimming
yr fingernails
you tip
their little

quarter-circles
onto a page
then open
the door

to dust them
onto the bent-
back-in-the-
breeze

grass silver
& green outside
where a leaf
lands at the same time

too.

## WEATHERED AIR

The least pattern
a splash of tan dye
between the blue lines of yr plate
thunder crackles & rumbles
blue-black sky
set off by the yellow walls of the terrace below –
that glow –
a storm's got its own rhythm & gossip
its own dialogue/monologue/diatribe
crackle answered by muffled boom
whispered thumping in lulls between.
Lay down a moment (I thought)
& slept. Woke to a small moth exploring the room
following past-present future-past
pouring round you
surrounding you now &
then now. And then now.
Fluid. Or not. Don't move. Sometimes …

>     lightly
>     entangled
>     in evening
>     breezes the
>
>     poisoned
>     hairs of the
>     Fair Nodding
>     Nettle ready

& what's
to touch among
grasses & wet
hedges downwind

of the possible
geese overhead
in v-formation
making for

a grazing patch
on the coast
sun-splashes
through cloud

in spring broken
chevrons descending
descending to the sea
&

towards evenings
long ago when the
lake would be flushed
with sunset colours

sending gentle
ripples towards
shore tiny waves
would break

on its edge
over short
tufted grasses or
little pockets of

pebbles & sand.
Now.

## FA SO LA

Music Appreciation, How to Write for a Living,
a rose is a raise is a ruse & a house to live in
now that you're dead and *useful* (being a reputation)
is this clear and crude enough?

Pivotal fulcra
                spinning dots
                              blended frames

shadow-light in light shadow, mica-glint & a
wind outside. Remember you know nothing.
And that nothing changes. Remember that
to slip past your shadow by the gable   love
food   death   sound of somebody talking
behind a hedge. Blurs, filaments. Is that you?

It's an early summer Sunday afternoon
branch-shadows moving a little in silence
then stopping then moving again on the wall
of a shed in a corner under some trees.

What date's today anyway   food   love   death
a child barking in a garden
it's a game (there's a response)
voiced voiceless fricatives & so on
goes the weave through the woven
& back   *bang-bang!*

Now shadows dislodge without a sound
& move again on the wall     sun disappears
clouds fade   re-form   love     food     death
talk-talk       breath-breath …

You can't deliver *everything* in a package
to the habit-acids whose chief delight is to
shade in small peripheral splotches until
at least until especially until as indirectly as
this she/where what you were saying

you were displaying *tenderness* as such
such that if we knew nothing
if nothing new were known now
would we exist?

## GLASS SHARD

Summer sparkles in your hair & through
black steel in the balcony from which
you'll make your first speech (political)
on this wild isle in about 1,000 years from
now flowing into dark child-eyes that watch
& track (this is history's little trick): listen –
throw time in the bin, they've changed it.
Does the species still exist? And the daughter
of the King of Greece will be yr bed companion
*a Dhónaill Óig*. Now. Black-white shadow-angles
in tiny streets down there slipping through
edge habitats a migrating loner-trickster,
through spinnies, shelter belts, plantations,
laneways, orchards, pools, marl pits,
gardens *a thin needle of ice beginning*
*to form, then an individual crystal*
*growing from the end of that needle*
*like a flower – look*  rootlets trick/le
down through separating earth-crumbs,
cuckoo-spit on nettle-stalk, conduits, gullies
of fire, whose flames lick & twist around
blackened, jagged rocks, rear & flick – is that
marram or wind-blown sea-grass yellow-green
in this light? Our keynote speaker this year will
deliver a paper entitled: "*Coffee Anyone? Ethics*
*and Late Modernism in the Developed World.*"
Big, open realisms – welcome to the house of
mirrors! Dark passageways, tiny, intricate
interconnections running this way, that.
To *take-say*: to deny, to *give-say*:  to promise,
to *say-say*: to love – forever & forever &
                forever.

# WIND

About-face:

into the splintering storm.
On the 2$^{nd}$ day of the 12$^{th}$ month
& a slap of Pathetic Fallacy too.
Is that a light in the sky?

Yes & no. And what's that
cramp in yr tummy, sonny?
It is the Force.

*Of course!*

Lips pursed, could be worse,
theory slamming theory to the ground
around which

in

    the

Great Crystal Mountain of Joy

that is yr Life

there is a whisper of

*je ne sais quoi*

(wha'?)

of something
difficult to pin down.

Penury, Sir?

Ah well. You take yr pen up & put it down again
sheets of glistening plastic hit & wrap tight
a tree-trunk on the street in the wind, black:

Inspector of Tiles

Ode to Springs

Comic Character from a Bavarian Folk Tale

The Basic Tones

The Wolves at Base

The Broken Glass.

Our philosopher Perspex, that all-knowing flipperty-
gibbet, Mickey Mouse.

## ON REFLECTION

Sea-water took sea-light in the
half-light & our boat slapped gently
by a little pier – *pippet, pipe, pip, pat* –
& I was alive, & you too, & young in
love & parenthood, & that was decades
ago now, in the Aegean, not experimenting,
not trying to, & definitely not bothering to be
the same old same old over again. Time & again.
*Ever* again. Here on this frail surface in
a copybook, braille, preoccupied, look,
your pocket-book with bits from your pockets
over the years in it, a coping book, *sin é*,
folded & wound round & the file crushed
open … o!

It's important to be the same they say
burgeoning population diminishing
planet vanishing species brittle laments
a flickering dance on thin ice
you might be asked to call 'life'
mapping the ceiling climbing the wall
painting your door in the zoo ho-hum
toodle-oo a whisper rippling along
the picket line (*tá blas na loinneoige
ar seo ná fuil?*) just play the game
whatever you do. Still.

I was humming what she thinks
I thought but I was wrong: *freedom?*
Happy the fly in the flue! So you're
an artist? Good. How do you do.

Just keep on scribbling, shaking
your fist, shouting, stamping, rattling
the bars, wasting our time & our energy,
boring your family, editors, enemies,
until a hammer hits the nail-head happily
spot on (& about time too) it's important
to try to grow up to be the same old riotous
One-Two – do you agree … you do?
Now!

## STILL LIFE

A single seed
arriving here years
ago making no
sound at all beside
your writing shed
become a
palm tree
little by little
(*I* should know)
now rattling
in the breeze now
jabbering about a bit
in agitation
beginning to
lean in the
calm now
years (*years*
we call them!)
years later shedding
& sending up
its apical bud
to the light.

Sudden screech of
a loosening bolt
on the gate
next-door scraping
the cracked path
& banging open
takes you
back abruptly back

a scrap of
language in a
lab to work on
peer into
open apart
then sound of
the damn thing
slamming again.
Breathe in.
Take note.
Sound of your
memories moving
sound of
thin ice
beginning to break
splashes of paint
quietly the code
your fingers
a page filling
& flowing
pleating descending
storks migrating
& at such great
height their calls
audible too
all the way
down to here
to you –
good lord!

You hold a
pine cone in
your hand, its

bristled feel
its woody
*sshish* when
you move your
fingers over
it – palm-print
ghost-touch –
working into
that area of
non-gabble
tilted towards
the light
& place it
with great care
there years later
swans' wings
overhead making
for the estuary
pushing pushing
down air
beside those
pieces of your
life you decide
might …

placing it
with care where
& placing it
seeds compacted
in the ribbed
undersoles
of your boots
herring gull

honeybee
& placing it with
care into what
the future's past
might look like
here beside those
pieces of your
life you decide
might (breathe in)
shiver of a
leaf on a breeze
(breathe breathe
take it & give
it back again) then
carefully to stamp
through time
& watch each
after-action
continuing
splash
blob
continuing
to here
afresh
into life
again.

# SONG

I took the rubbish to the rubbish hole
& poured it in knowing it had
been smouldering for some time back
struck a match with care   in the dry
season   feeling it must catch   cupping a hand
then despairing-hoping in its memory-
welter   this cold responsibility
to make it flare   to find & having found it
rebuild a shelter   love's ruins
love's memories   love's fire
flooding love's fire through each
fragment/tangible   too late   in
there   a crinkling paper corner
of just the A4 hope you need maybe to catch
being already dead it strikes you &
[dark corrugations intervene] Echo says ...
locked into the anthill the Normal Routine
carrying yr fleck in the tunnel
you wake, dreaming ... a long time ...

a sip of cold water in your throat
of an evening in a small town
in the hot south goes down
well – *tick!* – goes a bird on a cable
across a laneway – *tick-tick!* –
then another comes in
to feed its waiting nestlings there
making ready to fly
far down too   a slow sip of water
   the sobering water of life
   through to where

tight & high cupping the
globe moving in wind
as fire slips through sticks to the
upper reaches of the air in a nearby
garden   crackling/splintering   wings slap –
swoop – land – deliver – disappear –
a clock on a shelf, a magnifying glass
on a table over its clear wood-grain – *tock!* –
turbulence where a storm had been –
                                        down
far south they'll go –  swallow it –  again – and
put yr glass of coolness on the table down.

# GLIMPSE

Dusting air with yr right hand
to make what's left
right, & on a good day, better ...
Death – Sex – Memory – Regret –
throw the dice – what else next? Click.
Suddenly on a good day, young again,
you *get* it, left to right, left to right
itself into that dream of what's deemed
perfect, that dark inheritance you happen
to be heir to, that little trickling river of life ...
*le chiave, se notlolo, na heochracha.*
And write a poem about it.
In the summer of 1939 the poet Robert Lax
looked up into the sky of New York City
& saw jet-trails threading across from
building to building – dapple of windowglass –
jagged sirens – flags – pigeons – crowds –
& seeming to spell out he said, vividly, on
Patmos, fifty years later, a limber elder to this
young Irish eejit by the sea, the word *Pax*.

# SHUFFLE

A small house by a river, baby developing, dailiness, into the open air, flash of arrowing kingfisher, a stone bridge, a wide sky. Flow.

By chance I picked up an old copy of John Alcock's *The Kookaburra's Song* in Barcelona which led me to check Alcock's other work on the adaptive behaviours of species (one of my own adaptive behaviours), or now that I remember it, or she *helps* me to remember, M handed me that book in that bookshop in Barcelona that afternoon, & characteristically – the wide world's understated, under-estimated dances in their silence that implicate a music – she says now (to one who has lived with contingency all of his waking days) : *there is no such thing as chance!*

And so to begin again.

Early afternoon, sunshine after rain, on business at the bank, son in studio, a neighbour's noise – bang, whine of mechanical saw, planks & hammers – an insect glinting outside your window, fronds of a nearby palm that click in the breeze, dice hit the table, time, dailiness … flowing past, twisting, disappearing … the way a cat leaves a room, curling round a doorjamb into open, un-frameable air.

And so, to begin again.

# DA CAPO

I knew you thirty years ago.
You passed with your wife &
child & friend busy, happy, chatting,
laughing, snapping yr fingers, ah.
I passed. We passed. *You* passed.
You'd been moving on to the
*Reward Storage Terminal* all that time,
I'd been making for the periphery,
I didn't know. Cut. Viscosity. Sunlight
on a leaf. The weight of that …

  this must be
  the way
  back to that
  persistent

  ball at the
  brink of ignition
  from the crest of

  regret lest we forget
  that old chestnut
  (& when they're gone

  they're gone) – tested –
  that piece of
  darkness – come in! –

  (*forget?!*) – well –
  down – tilting – turning –
  landing – the way

the leaves
leave the trees
in visible waves

while
whispers of litter
build in the

little breezes
between this
& this darkness

on your desk
on the open
surface of it thus.

This is a *poem* right? Cup hands
to see. Our keynote speaker's paper on
*'Mild Hangover & the Urban Muse.'*
This is good. This is not good. No ifs
& buts, smug as a bug in a mug, vivid
splash of blossom, dark alleyway in a city,
where am I? You tell me.

# REFRACTION

To sip this
bit of coffee
all the way
from Bolivia
hot to yr tentative lips
to here today

step

*that* kind of world.
To try a few
cul de sacs
because …

because nobody
knows or cares
& a strong smell
of lingering cliché
curls up treetrunks
suckering sweet sap.

Place Pain there
Love beside it
& here Pure Pleasure
& here too Exploration

    *the first mark*
        *(burst bark)*
    *leaf hit leaf*

*remember to let go*
            *the clinging storyline*
*of yr*
      (from the other hand)
                    *yr grief*

from the other hand too Dark
can't be far away & Shock & Stone
& Acorn Cup its growth-surround its
ghost of power its piece of beautiful
future mapped

      *grey sac –*
              *fly trap –*
      *dust gathering*
                *on a plastic pot*

place One-Hard-Look on the table
*take it in* then yr hands & yr hands' work
*take it all in* a stone on a path
is a stone on a path: step over it.
Count yr steps. Remember them.

Wisps of steam.

# MIRRORING

In this garden a tree flowers
against a wall.

A wall. This. A mass of blossom
against an old stone wall.

A conversation turns
out to be a monologue
cogs & sprockets
branches & lichens.

One foot on the ground, two:
plan – wish – sift – remember.

This laneway that once was a road
now goes (you can ask) "nowhere".

A wall.

Where a little dust separates.

Drops into place. Listen.

The danger of what happens retold becoming
quotation impeded by grace words being
pretty bad at this quote me on this
the shadow teaching the light the light
it was a happy life
to carve out dials quaintly, point by point.

## NATURE OF THINGS

Follow the branches as they bifurcate
& watch the whole thing blossom.
What are the primal building blocks
& how do they fit together?
Follow the branches as they bifurcate
& watch the whole thing blossom,
the 'steady voice of realism',
the crystal pyramids of illusion,
the gaps between ethics & success,
perks optional. Know what I mean?

A rain so light, a little whisper,
leaf-brush, the merest whisper,
how say it, listen, listen in, how,
light flickers, children's tree-house
creaks, a distant gate closes, doves
too, distant, too, a carpenter's
hammering, a van's reversing bleep …

Whose is that big *thing* out there, that
*Art*, bulky, colourful, solid, odd,
new to this place, what on earth …
(How much is it, Mister, how much &
  what's it for? Yeh what's it *for* Mister?
  What's it do? Is it yours? Didja make it?
  Didja? Can I kick it? Yeh? It's *lovely*!)
tiny banded globes, spiralling cilia,
flashed signals, transparent worms
studded with phosphorescent lights,
darks, shocks of vivid in little twisted
caves, tentacle, proboscis, furrowed shell.

## ABACUS

A piece of spider-silk floating from
the ceiling down onto the page
of my book changing (clap) *if the sun
& moon are* (clap) changing *both pulling
the Earth & its water in the same line then*
(clap-clap) what happens, changing
what happens: nose in a book, head
in the clouds. Why did money
arise simultaneously in vastly different
cultures two & a half thousand years ago
& on the dot? (Wrong question?) *Click*
go the sliding pellets *click-click*
on the timeline: how do you write your/
*why* do you write your history & how
frame it? Your *what*? I read 'wholefood' as
'wolf-food' & realize … Now then. Time
for a coffee. Out into the wilds we go.
To classify things, circular objects, small
globular objects, things which have a mouth –
bags, boxes & the like – of chairs &
sheets of paper, for various animals, parts of
the body, articles of clothing & ships,
for things that are grasped by a handle –
fans, knives – number, things & people,
number them now, one by one by one,
in the building of the world in words.

## TRADITIONAL AIR

I put the book down.
Here we are – that's
the storm, listen
it into you –

it blooms, cascades,
thank it (I do) &
picked a hammer up –
tap-tap – thinking –

watching as the Nail.
Goes. In. One little
plank meets another,
& fits. Do come round

    again this evening
      won't you?

## TIME'S TABLE

Woke
into the adventure
out of the blue

wherein reflections
on glass, water etc
inscrutable doubleness

in the background radiation
a song they say can …
well keep you going

watching the graspers grasp
noting past passing past
into past – tra-la –

*tiredness* as a working method
matching the scratching beast at the
fence. If the grammar is upside-

down it pebbles nutrition apples
rubbing 25% together waves
splash door bed ceiling &

this must be the floor tilting
down & what's that glowing
in the dark tacked to the

billboard outside your window
that tilts too? Thousands of
people around the world

are writing their poetry
in their own languages
right now.

No offence meant. In languages
that are not crushed, that is.
Pocked, porous.

Lips that met your lips
that loved you once are
silent now. Sing that.

And slightly askew. Note
that too. A lovely dress once
touched echoes a touching

address much loved once
mirror-seeming through your
dreaming head again fold on

fold (now) that taps another into
place in whatever lingo you
choose to brew yr news in now.

Mist. Loss of feeling on the left side,
increase of insight on the right, right?
That insect on your finger probing

for blood, your agitation on the page
showing glowing readiness to
follow these collapsing dances,

these little *here-I-ams*, mind
brittle, world bright.
Sweat that one out.

# LANDSCAPE

*Enough is enough* is written on the sand
ahead of the incoming tide – I'm in front
of my footsteps, just: what about you?
Nobody wants to know (are you a hatter?) –
love, money, affection, esteem: I'll settle
for a piece of fresh apple to chew. Enough
is enough. Blackbirds. A dance is a. Call

me back. This pen-point raised to … ah … strike
that match, its flame, its sap-drop glistening
down its length as the fire-lick progresses, then
out. Black. Step. HELLO. I'm on the train.
Writing, I put my foot down though, do you?
I'll call you back is the beginning of the
Blackbird Song you've been taking steps

towards completion for some time now
which in every way is the opposite I feel
of The Poem of the White Bird by the Seashore.
"His father was a hatter of good reputation."
What does "now" mean now anyway? I'm on
the train. I'll call you back. Dust floats from a
skylight, one caught grain, then several – down –

grey, gold – to the left then to the right while
two crows come through it to the other side
among the dogs of art, & their cronies & ballads.
Which albeit some of vs do lyk well & think
our toung thereby much bettred yet do strangers
therefor carry the farre lesse opinion therof,
some saying it is of itself no language at all

> but the scum of several.

*An Ceangal*

Wind blows & the leaves yellow & fall & time
it seems time when you turn your neck &
head is slowed – *wait-wait-wait-for-me-me-me!*
go the gulls over the bay – as each leaf in its
individual glow-sphere falls (this is that poetry
thing going on again isn't it) falls & dances on
       the blown bright grass below.

# CADENZA

then wedged a long
pole between ceiling
& floor with care a
newelpost carved in

heartwood   tricky   every
surface out of true (so
what's new?) (sunlight is
on things) (trees windows

angular niches pillars
lenses utensils fabrics
mirrors chrome ceramic –
surface over surface –

transparent/opaque) & a
homemade plumbline  curved
light/dark vertical con-
volvulus a bee a beetle

a caterpillar on a stem
for the children straight
up let them centre this
house for us the eye too

    (light)

    thanks.

a single handclap from a long-
drawn-out slow-motion segment of
applause that slips along quite

nicely thank you just below the
surface (of yr [idea of yr] life)
(was that a gunshot?) (what?!)

celebrating – or just cerebrating –
& sometimes – oh yes – taking
    note.

   *cover. darling.*
   is it.
   (gotcha)


   .

# BLUEBELLS IN A WOOD: WALTZ

but then we

the most

we had the

wonderful

most

ful

the most wonderful

time

# Notes

Irish language:

p 55: *A Tilted Mirror*, stanza 7: "is skittle bawn morgay on": *'s citeal bán mar ghé ann*: & a white (ie enamel) kettle like a goose in it (ie the spout reminds the child-like observer of a goose's long, curved neck), from *Cúl an Tí* (The Backyard) by Séan Ó Ríordáin. The poet is referring to the contents of a dump in a backyard. This fragment written in "English" here to bring to mind the dividing membrane between the two languages.

p 64: *Arc: idir na*: among the

p 65: *Arc: idir na daoinibh duarca*: among the miserable people, from Dáibhí Ó Bruadair's [c1625 – 1698] darkly, brilliantly acerbic *mairg nach fuil 'na dhubhthuata*.

p 89: *Glass Shard:* Lines 8/9: *Is beidh 'níon rí na Gréige ina céile leapa leat,* from *Dónall Óg*, trad. song.

p 92: *On Reflection*, stanza 1: *sin é*: that's it

p 92: *On Reflection*, stanza 2: *tá blas na loinneoige ar seo ná fuil?*: this has the feel of a chorus, doesn't it?

p 100: *Glimpse: na heochracha*: the keys (*se notlolo* = the keys, in Sesotho, pronounced: 'say knot-lulu')

p 114: *Landscape: An Ceangal:* [literally 'the tie' or 'knot']: L'envoi

§

p 54: *Imprints*: Adapted from: paragraph 1: Tristan Gooley, '*Wild Signs & Star Paths*'. Paragraph 2: Ken Edwards, '*A Grey Area*'. Paragraph 3: Agota Kristof '*The Third Lie*'.

p 72: *Canvas*: The opening stanza from an obituary of the painter Gillian Ayres. The 2$^{nd}$ stanza, a distorted snippet of a translation of the Anglo-Saxon fragmentary poem known as 'The Ruin' from the *Exeter Book*; version by Billy Mills

p 100: *Glimpse*: Contrails over NYC in 1939? A narrative fold, or a trick of memory?

# Contents

| | |
|---|---|
| Tracking | 7 |
| Mirrors | 9 |
| Air | 13 |
| Earth | 25 |
| Dice | 29 |
| Song | 31 |
| Scales | 33 |
| Being There | 35 |
| Translating | 36 |
| Look | 38 |
| Night Studio | 40 |
| Chequered Air | 41 |
| A Grey Area | 43 |
| Tabled | 44 |
| Do Re Mi | 48 |
| Chink | 49 |
| Self-Portrait as Oddity | 51 |
| Imprints | 54 |
| A Tilted Mirror | 55 |
| Cards | 59 |
| Arc | 63 |
| Pitch | 66 |
| Tuning | 68 |
| Lullaby | 70 |
| Canvas | 72 |
| Frame | 74 |
| Map 1 | 75 |
| Map 2 | 77 |
| Map 3 | 78 |
| Working | 79 |

| | |
|---|---|
| Mapping | 81 |
| As the Cat | 82 |
| Weathered Air | 84 |
| Fa So La | 87 |
| Glass Shard | 89 |
| Wind | 90 |
| On Reflection | 92 |
| Still Life | 94 |
| Song | 98 |
| Glimpse | 100 |
| Shuffle | 101 |
| Da Capo | 102 |
| Refraction | 104 |
| Mirroring | 106 |
| Nature of Things | 107 |
| Abacus | 108 |
| Traditional Air | 109 |
| Time's Table | 110 |
| Landscape | 113 |
| Cadenza | 115 |
| | |
| Bluebells in a Wood: Waltz | 119 |
| | |
| *Notes* | 120 |

*Author photo: James Keating.*

https://mauricescullysite.wordpress.com

www.ingramcontent.com/pod-product-compliance
Lightning Source LLC
Chambersburg PA
CBHW031354160426
43196CB00007B/810